SHEARSMAN

113 & 114

WINTER 2017 / 2018

GUEST EDITOR ISSUE 113 / 114
KELVIN CORCORAN

EDITOR
TONY FRAZER

Shearsman magazine is published in the United Kingdom by
Shearsman Books Ltd
50 Westons Hill Drive
Emersons Green
BRISTOL   BS16 7DF

Registered office: 30-31 St James Place, Mangotsfield, Bristol BS16 9JB
(this address not for correspondence)

www. shearsman.com

ISBN 978-1-84861-541-0
ISSN 0260-8049

Subscriptions and single copies

Current subscriptions—covering two double-issues, each around 100 pages in length—cost £16 for delivery to U.K. addresses, £18 for the rest of Europe (including the Republic of Ireland), and £21 for the rest of the world. Longer subscriptions may be had for a pro-rata higher payment. North American customers will find that buying single copies from online retailers in the U.S.A. or Canada will be cheaper than subscribing. This is because airmail postage rates in the U.K. have risen rapidly, whereas copies of the magazine are printed in the U.S.A. to meet demand from online retailers there, and thus avoid the transatlantic mail and its onerous costs.

Back issues from n° 63 onwards (uniform with this issue) cost £8.95 / $16 through retail outlets. Single copies can be ordered for £8.95 direct from the press, post-free within the U.K., through the Shearsman Books online store, or from bookshops. Issues of the previous pamphlet-style version of the magazine, from n° 1 to n° 62, may be had for £3 each, direct from the press, where copies are still available, but contact us for a quote for a full, or partial, run.

Submissions

Shearsman operates a submissions-window system, whereby submissions may only be made during the months of March and September, when selections are made for the October and April issues, respectively. Submissions may be sent by mail or email, but email attachments—other than PDFs—are not accepted. We aim to respond within 3 months of the window's closure, i.e. all who submit *should* hear by the end of June or December, although for recent issues we have often taken a month longer.

This issue has been set in Bembo with titling in Argumentum.
The flyleaf is set in Trend Sans.

Contents

John Levy

An Abstract Painting in the Sky

I'm thinking of beginning an anthology
of poems I like
about death. Just

for fun. I read
a very good one yesterday.
Yesterday is dead

maybe. Some poets can write breezy
poems and all
I have to do and want to do is

be with them. I can live
with that. I'm not thinking of
making an anthology of those

pieces, though. Yesterday a gila
monster walked on the path around our
back yard that I had taken too. I was taken

with it (not sure of gender) and
for the first time in my life watched
a gila monster go down into a hole.

An opening, under a tree, perhaps
dug by yet another. The gila
not–really–a–monster–

anymore–than–I–am so maybe it is too
shot
a forked tongue out about

every six to 12 seconds (a
guess, I wasn't timing). It's one of those many
lives who have only legs. I am happy

with my arms. Would I mind
being a fish? An anthology of poems
about body parts

is another idea to trash. I dreamed
last night I was in Phoenix in
the house where I lived as a child, though

I was a man and thousands
of birds began to cry so I grabbed
my camera and went out the front door to

see all those birds. They
weren't there. It was night. I
looked up. One fairly small

somewhat circular patch in the sky
with wobbling colored borders grew
somewhat bigger then

luminous patterns within it brightened
while another area of sky started to
blossom even more brightly and a third it was

the end of the world I
watched the sky announce
as if every living creature's death would

come in about one minute after this night
sky finished turning into a fabulous complex
vivid abstract painting. I woke, it was one

a.m. If there is an afterlife what
kind of anthology of thoughts feelings
moments vision could and would

be edited by whom or what and
would it be more than a sequence
in another time, could it be somehow an all-

at-once everything-you-lived-through-and-
became. And could it include
become, a became/become

neverending arrival that would have to be
eternal? An eternal something-
or-other? Easier for me to imagine

reincarnation, as if I learned
that concept in a brochure
entitled AFTERLIFE FOR DUMMIES

that starts, perhaps
in a nit-picky manner, by asking
what's AFTER doing there

if it's more a THEN-THEN-THEN
chain of lives. The lives can't be
unspecific, the way death threatens.

Three First Lines of Lee Harwood Poems
Plus Three First Lines of Gael Turnbull Poems

The dreadful loneliness
Bears dance to the music, slowly, awkwardly
The scent – bog myrtle

It was a good boat, never better,
glitter of what's far off,
It's raining on the brussels sprouts.

Shitember

She weighs nothing she believes. Flames
patiently wait, she tells herself, night
spat out the moon and morning.
She rides another bus, watches
how other women display breasts,
hears despair in passers-by's

footsteps. She
is going to work. She
answers calls for someone else all
day long
she weighs nothing and flames
patiently wait. The office joker reminds her

of an insect. The panhandler on the corner
of snow falling in summer. The world
outside the window surrounds the telephone wires
stretched from one pole to another.
She told her stuffed animals, one-by-one, to have
good dreams before her father

turned off the bedroom light. Now he
weighs nothing underground, ash
atop ash in the cremation
urn. She, too, chose
like her father to work among the dogs and wolves, as
her mother used to call

her father's co-workers. Her mother, who
named months Shitly or Shitember or
Shituary or Shitust. Her father would laugh.
Her husband has no idea. She chose him
after she told him they could live
in a jar with fireflies and he chuckled. She

chose him when he didn't grimace
when she spoke of waiting to
sleep together until the end of Shitust and
he asked why and she said Because.
He was willing to wait. She
sees it all as waiting.

Seven First Lines by Emily Dickinson
Plus Seven First Lines by Frederick Seidel

I hide myself within my flower,
I tried to think a lonelier Thing
I felt a Cleaving in my Mind —
I felt a Funeral, in my Brain,
I felt my life with both my hands
I cautious, scanned my little life —
Perhaps I asked too large —

I am pushing the hidden
My own poetry I find incomprehensible.
I shaved my legs a second time,
I stick my heart on a stick
I've never been older.
I attend a concert I can ruin
But we are someone else. We're born that way.

Julie Maclean

'I have always imagined that Paradise will be a kind of library."

'Nothing is built on stone; all is built on sand...'

'To fall in love is to create a religion that has a fallible god.'
—Jorge Luis Borges

He is wearing a dead man's suit

It smells of ash, Paris,
from his last trip there
in '63.

His hair is the hair
of a melting man
run into his skull
clump of a clown each side.

He wears a tie out of respect.
His wife does not like it.
Too pussy grey she thinks.
She'd like him to wear a red one
loosely tied at his noose neck.
Baboon's arse of a knot, no doubt.

She is Alti Plana at the heart.
Well, he thinks she is.

How could he know. She will not let him
near her sun-kissed, air-dried dunes.
Says he is a limp vine. Not a real man.
referring to his pen of course—

slough of a green snake.
He is hung like the full-fat moon
in his mother's eyes.

Montezuma huge.
King of the sand cathedrals.

He carries his manifesto with him always.
It tells him to be fair.

Be fair. Be a writer.

His wife does not agree
even in translation.

He carries her on his arm.
She never liked being a handbag.

He thinks she's unable to read him.
He always loved being a book.

Doppelgänger at Skara Brae

I saw you at the Ness of Brodgar
hair of the Celt hint of the mullet
fair-skinned pink in the wind
You were quarrying rock along the peninsula   Oliver's mane
                  swooshing

It's the age
when forts are found in dig diaries along lines of religion
like yours at the altar of cigarettes Guinness a cup of tea
carbon dated to last century

Chapel samples show your devotion
to the family catholic the nap
several times removed from Eire /another cigarette out the back/

In a stony zeitgeist grooved in Orkney
your double marvels at Arcadian loft-lines radiating south
to the land of death   remarking how small those henge stones
on the plain
that open stage ripe for blood and ceremony

Looking down structures 1,8,11
he notes hearths, doors,
carved whalebone
and the beauty of the number 3

Controlled spaces like your living room
conceal a solitary chair at another shrine
BBC   Match of the Day
this choreography of rites
tied to land, leather and air
weapons of power   unearthed in your sacred HQ

I step up to ponder
ceramics painted red   sedge warblers and ex-girlfriends in
                                                    pictures
on your wall   white tiles in your marvellous
new bathroom   red towels in your rituals of dawn/dusk
                                                    landscapes
      face to face in the mirror of your ancestors   land of the living

each morning crossing the threshold to Stones of Stenness and
                                                structure 10
portals to the dead
relic hairdryer   preserved in a bee meadow

Crossing to Caerleon

I vow to be Roman again
From a drone's eye I look so elliptical
so planned and curving
not a kink to be seen
even a wall keeping deplorables out

I am in the Museum of Facepaint now
dipping three fingers into my special pot
of black goat cream to soften my English-wintered skin
Below the guild hall of glass and piping
I am in the arena and someone meaty is coming for me
fists in gusts   so I'm off

In my one-person skiff
clay chalk and gravel fan out
in perfectly straight lines
from the ferry across the murky Channel
I fling coins to the gods for a safe passage

How noble we centurions of mathematical equation
breastplates and strappy sandals
full bore into pillage and victory

Oh those Welsh resisters
Songsters thick-necked hairy-arsed Silurians
Usk-bound boys of lowland occupation
with sheep
abristle with iron and hormones

How swarthy and short they are
with their woolly hair of curly quality
baying for blood and bread

We trample them like tussocks   Hear us roar

Nostra victoria est!

Ballantyne's Rascal on Wiki

hikes into Wewak to pick pockets
takes booty to the spirit house.

To reinforce his manhood
he is told *Never kiss a girl*

for fear of ingesting menstrual flow
and turning limp as a leaf and secretly prays

he is not chosen to be dropped
into the post hole and sacrificed alive

under a dressed Banyan leaving subterranean
remains for the uninitiated.

When his time arrives he is pleased to be
cut with a broken bottle in the pattern of a crocodile.

A blade of sedge wedged into his glans
splitting his thing four ways.

He wears tribal scars with a wide grin of Betel-stained teeth
interrupted by the occasional nub of PK chewing gum

and when fully done is able to bleed a pig
leaving no mess not a skerrick of gristle.

As a new man he will carve chicken on Sunday
keep the pond clean and mow the lawn when he can

with that special ship-wrecked look
as a man does when he has one.

Helen Tookey

On the Black Canal

Your boat is moored on the black canal
and the woman is playing the cello for you,

long low notes the colour of crows' wings.
You are a sound-box, air vibrates inside your bones

as each note elongates, a dark expanse –
are you under her protection, or is it a baffle

she draws around you, words becoming lost
in the rasp of bow against wire, your skull

full of overtones. Where were you trying to go that day
as you crossed the fields when the planes came,

droning low, forcing you down with the weight
of the sound in your head – you lay it seemed

for hours, pressed to the earth, unable to move
till the sound cleared, the weight eased

from your bones and you ran, away from
the terror of air, the fields' aphasic spaces.

Where were you going? You can't remember, and now
you're moored in the long box of your boat, and the woman

is playing the cello for you, the sound closing
over your head like black water, like crows' wings.

Episode

On the fourth-floor landing of a municipal building
a woman slips a man's hand inside her shirt, places it

against her breast. Her nipple stiffens
between his fingers and she stares wordlessly

over his shoulder, out of the staircase window.
It is three o'clock on a December afternoon

and the light is fading, the cars have their headlights on.
In the schoolyard below the children are waiting

to be collected. They are calm and unthinking
because their lives are governed by others' decisions.

The man has to leave to meet his daughter
so the moment breaks and falls away – a small misstep

in the construction of a theory, a move in a game
with no explanatory power.

The woman neatens her shirt. The man puts his hands
in his pockets. In the schoolyard, each child

is duly returned to a parent. The afternoon fails.

Halb Null

It occurred to me to ask the time. She said *Halb null*. Half an hour to zero. How did it get so late? We had done nothing, only dallied in the café in the square, eating bread and artichokes, using up time to no purpose, and yet with a long journey to make. Halb null, and we had not even set out!

There were road blocks, long queues of traffic out of the city. At a standstill alongside a wide flat field, we watched circus performers rehearsing, tossing fire-sticks to each other in complicated patterns and interweavings. Sometimes they missed their catches, laughed as the fire-sticks fell harmlessly at their feet. It was late and they were only rehearsing, there was no sense of urgency or concern among them. But for us, time had slipped through our fingers, it seemed that we might never get back.

City of Departures

When I stepped out of the house the morning air held rain, the scent of it, the taste. The light was bruised and yellowish. A blackbird was singing, very clearly, his song amplified by the coming rain. The scene felt familiar, already lived-through. The caption was *Morning in the city of departures*. I was walking through narrow streets close to the docks, under the piers of bridges, through brick archways. The cobblestones were wet and I had on no shoes. There had been a railway accident, journeys were disrupted or rendered impossible. You didn't appear and yet you were present, if only in the feeling of missed connections. You were there in the sense of having spoken a vital word to me and then departed, leaving me wandering the wet quaysides holding the word I couldn't use, a bright coin in the wrong currency.

Daragh Breen

Tarot

When the weathervane dealt the cards
Jack Ketch got dealt the barge,
and in its slow, coopered wake
it trailed the bird-shells of all
the spring-eggs that he'd crushed
during his hooded days.

The reddleman and the pig-bleeder
will come at dawn to redden the skies
as the barge hatches him in last night's
mud, his white body stretched like a
badger's back, forever scorched by that
falling star that fell across its ancestor's spine.

Syzygy

Between the twin black souls
of the rabbit's eyes
the moon swam
into the shadow of the Earth
and the rats spilled their guts
hanging them out to dry
as the hares slipped their skins
and paraded on the stilts
of their hind legs

and the old women of the village
emptied their chamber pots
over the yew trees,

the Witching Act having been
superseded by the universe,
for when everything is aligned
nothing is right,
every single thing is in the shadow
of the shadow of the shadow.

Victorian

I

Out in his cobbled backyard
the Reverend Jack Russell watches
a goldfinch prepare for its own funeral,
muted by the stacks of ghost-white
dog hair that its snatches from the ground.

He has been breeding for a few seasons now,
miniaturising at every step, unpacking
the Russian Doll of a fox-hunting dog
from each of the discarded ghosts.
Every dawn and dusk he has watched
the local foxes steal their red cloven way
across the fields, the tinderbox
of their nerves scurrying for sanctuary
now that the covenant has been betrayed.

II

A fox slid out of the ivy hedging up ahead
and stalled to stare at our two dogs, their
leads harnessing them to a different world
as a brief flame of sensation shimmered
between all three, a flicker of startled memory.

Napkins of cloud were dragged through the
pewter ring of the moon, napkin tied to
napkin of night being hurried through, as a
startle of crows harassed each other through
a child's broken drum and the cot lurched like
a ship in hardening ice
                              – the nursery had been
disturbed, and all three had fled their disrupted
Eden.

III

One of the dogs came back out of the ditch
head tilted upwards and proudly panting,
his mouth stuffed with the ball of a staring
rabbit's head, its ears smoothly stiff,
a medieval shuttlecock,
perfectly and neatly severed,
the veins neatly trimmed,
as if the fox had just unscrewed and
discarded it like a doll's head

of the kind that the same fox had dismantled
the winter previous, stealing about
the frozen fields in its clothes,
the frilled hems being distracted and
harassed by every thorned hedgerow.

Steve Ely

The Ballad of Jack Ross

Ross	*You're not a patch on your brother, are you?*
P.M. Walters	*[crestfallen] No, I suppose not.*
Ross	*You'd be no use at all if it wasn't for him. In fact, there's only one better back than A.M.*
P.M. Walters	*Who?*
Ross	*Me.*

Jack Ross was born on Gorgie Road
in a rat-hole tenement,
water running down the walls
three-months arreared of rent.

Young Jack came out kicking,
some say he never stopped,
from Bernard's Well to the Dancing Club
he tripped and hacked and chopped.

Fleet as a racing snap-dog,
game as a scarred Blue Paul,
he dogged the pitch from box-to-box
in rush and ruck and maul.

Sharp as a border sheepdog,
wise as a hoar deerhound,
he strode the field and ran the game
for Saturday's sneaking pound.

King Cotton came a-calling,
and trebled his backhand cash;
Jack headed South to terrorise
those milk-sop Sassenachs.

His teeth were green as spat catarrh
and through them clenched he'd hiss

threats and murder at his foes
till their knickers streaked with piss.

He hobbled Billy Bassett,
snapped James Brown like a stick,
kicked Nevill Cobbold in the nuts
and tenderised his dick.

No forward could get past him,
he smashed down everyone,
but Sudell would not pay his worth—
so he signed for Everton.

But Anfield's up-front hundred pounds
bought only a single season,
for a hundred more from sour Sudell
helped loyal Jack see reason.

But Jack was not the man he was,
there was something on his chest
and after every match a coughing-fit
left blood streaked down his vest.

Sudell sent him to Madeira
that he might recuperate
and get back to his blinding best—
and staunch the bleeding from the gate.

But Gorgie's blight had rotted deep
and Jack was too far gone;
he died in his Fishwick terrace
at the age of thirty-one.

Ten thousand lined the pouring streets
to see Jack's grand cortège,
and bowed their dripping, hatless heads
as the mournful piper played.

And every mill-hand's running dog
threw back its head and howled
at the tumbril's stately passage
to St. Stephen's clay-gouged goal.

And the curtains closed on Fishwick's streets,
the blinds on Gorgie Road
and Jock devoured by England's earth,
into Hell enrolled.

And the curtains closed at Tynecastle,
and closed on Deepdale's stage,
where ten thousand mill-hands, Bill Sudell,
roared applause—and wage.

Their lucred approbation
rocked Satan's fiery gaol
and raptured Gorgie's ghostly-gun
back to Preston's golden 'dale.

Where sovereigns and brown envelopes
were pressed in pallid palm—
'Encore, Jack! Take a bow, son!
In our grief, you were our balm.'

Jubilate Messi

'For there is a note added to the scale, which the Lord hath
made fuller, stronger and more glorious.'
           (Christopher Smart, *Jubilate Agno*)

I will rejoice in Lionel Andrés Messi; for he leaps before the Lord like
David, and his joy is uncovered: *Let the rain streak bright in the flaring*
floodlights, Empire's phosphorescent rainbow arching like a cat.

For he is brave and boyish, with the dark eyes of the pit-dog and the shy mouth of the wolf: *Let him shear the sheep of the bloody devil, pluck the condors of Falange.*

For the cunning Right Hand and gloried Left Foot are but gifts from the finger of God: *Let left triumph over right, the shin-snapping lunges of Goikoetxea and Ramos, the death-dives of Videla.*

For cocaine and cortisone, Diego's duende, Thatcher and Shilton's woes: *Let Castro and Kirchner join in applause for Azteca's avenging viveza.*

For Jack flies over Stanley, Belgrano is coffined at sea: *Let Butcher and Beardsley, Fenwick and Reid be ruthless as Rattín, savage as Samuel, brutal as Batista.*

For he dusts down and demurs not, nor will he fall to foul or faking: *Let them be honest as the horse and humble as the ass.*

For he has the grace of Garrincha and the guts of Gascoigne; Zola's zest, the balance of Best, and Bergkamp's balmy touch: *Let Der Bomber give praise, and Henry's heart, leap like the lenten roe.*

For Garrincha lies dead in his drunkard's grave, Best slaughtered, Gazza mortal: *Let maté be prepared and neapolitan schnitzel, Milanello's pasta e pollo.*

For Guevara fought with Simba in Congo, El Proceso v. Task Force and those disappeared: *Let Cuito Cuanavale live long in the song, how the FAR pulled the teeth of Die Groot Krokodil.*

For though Sunyol is murdered and Guernica plaint, Galtieri and gauleiters—dead: *Let the cloud-crested noontide soar albiceleste, eventide crimsoned and blue.*

For the lepers shall inherit the mower-striped Earth: *Let the grass spurt green in the urchinned precincts, the playgrounds plunge with boys.*

For Alves knows his duty and gives him the ball: *Let Andrés and Xavi and Pedro attend, Sorín, Saviola, Juan Román Riquelme.*

For Balons and titles are but nets of the Tempter: *Let the spirit flow with joy.*

For he spurts from the butchers like blood-jet, fearless as Fangio, fierce as Gardel : *Let the bobbles and rebounds fall to his fast feet forever.*

Non licet omnibus adire Corinthum

There is no fixed rule defining a member's qualifications, but there is an unwritten law confining election to Old Public School Boys or members of a university.
       B.O. Corbett, Thame Grammar School, Oriel College,
       Corinthian F.C. & England.

The myriad viands of Golden Mile
scanted their idiote palates—professing
codfish-in-batter and chipped potatoes,
the athletes had swaggered off tiddly-om-pom,
to gorge on their monkey-gland, magneton
soul food, muscled-up pygmies dining to giants,
pot-bellied on Dublin porter.
                              At length,
crisp linen, the Palatine Hotel;
oysters off the half-shell, '61 Cliquot.
The porne at table flirting with Cunners;
int you a size, Sir. Cunliffe sportive;
I suppose I am, my dear—a sly glance
at Charlie—*well, all the girls say so.*
Oakers rolling his eyes, Joe looking down
at his shellfish; the fellowship falling about.
A warm un an all. Cunners raising his eyebrows
and turning away, tapping the ash
from his cigar; a dozen Campaspes
in Mayfair apartments, unnumbered
country-house hetairai.

              Players banging
the plate glass window, ruddy as rustics —
Tower Ballroom to grab some birds.
The gentlemen rose and adjusted their cummerbunds.
Oakers and Joe retiring. There was drinking,
then dancing, Cunners and Charlie, Tinsley Lindley,
stripping the silks of champagne showgirls
in five-guinea suites at the Grand Hotel:
straight-shot Steve and Nudger Needham,
dropping five-bob bloomers and rusty arseholes
against the stanchions of the Central Pier.

*The gentlemen amateurs of Corinthian F.C. and their professional teammates
in the England XI share a night out in Blackpool after an international.*

26

Cathy Dreyer

Form

Away down the field sits a blackbrown hare.
With the sun behind her, she's a shadow,
a woodcut silhouette, the ideal hare,

holding herself ideally still, as though
she died years ago, or is a picture
of herself, already faded, as though

a sudden light caused over-exposure,
too many lux seconds when the shutter
opened. A moment's over-exposure

and the light-sensing surfaces smudge her
into mud and crushed blacks, important bright
areas are washed out. She's a smudge, her

highlights blown out, or zoomed in on too tight.
You can't see her, though she's still in plain sight.

Happy ever after: Beauty and the Beast

The Beast therefore behaved in beastly ways,
demanding *filet mignon* cooked *à point*, eg, or
coq au vin with crudités and seared legume,
to tempt his gullet. He made her scrub the whole
white bath the length of its enamel snow, not just
smear the tide mark of their slurry with a cloth.
She must use the brand new Hoover on the dark
wool carpets that he chose, going into every corner,
and this was after she had wiped her shoes, properly,

before she jangled up the glass-cased
steel stairway, he'd had constructed
to a brutalist design (which had *brought out*,
not scarred) the Grecian detailing
of the 1860s villa. (This handily allowed
its lucrative conversion into four attractive flats.)
Then sex of course, and every night, though
only in traditional position.
                                        But most of all,
he required access to the index of the book
of her, so he could to look up every gesture
in her lexicon, testing it for truth and for consistency,
not caring if he broke the spine.
   When she
denied him, he would sneer and smash their
mirrors. He'd say his mother warned him
that his Beauty was a money-wort, those
dirty shiksas being all the same. What a
mug he'd been! Then Beauty cried and
smoked the cigarettes he hated, sitting
on her side of their big bed (which had developed a
sad hillock in between the coastal hollows
of their nightly separation) unable to
construct an answer which did not
incriminate her, because, although his
mother had it wrong, Beauty's truth was
ugly. On the rebound from a chinless,
older lover, she had revelled in the drama
of the Beast's repeated threats to *end it all*
if she refused his ring. He bought a canister
of gas, his green eyes bugged and bulging,
teeth jagged in the red and roaring
cavern of his mouth—*I'll do it! I don't want
to live without you!*—the matching horror
of their parents—these were satisfying consolations.
Beast's money? A convenience, not more.

Of course, Beauty could not tell him that and so,
in another end, she left the flat forever, the baby
on her hip, the toddler's sweaty hand in hers. She
took nothing with her. Nothing that was his, or theirs—
to show him, and his mother. She knew that he'd be
fair, he wasn't just a beast, not the *heinous Christocidal*
Jew her father rang into her ears when bride and groom
returned from Scotland, her white boots (Courrèges)
already streaked with pavement dust, her silken,
hooded mini-dress gone grey with creases. It would
be alright. She told herself that Beast was only partly
beast. At least, she knew, he wouldn't let his children
live in damp and bronchial poverty, would he?

What is bitcoin?

Bitcoin is the currency of *don't trust, verify,* it floats on digitally
transparent seas, as if the old Directory Enquiries included every call
you've made and what you said, indelible in public ledgers, and not
just people's numbers—

So that on the day you clamber from the clammy flat in Tufnell Park,
to bask on Highgate's gracious balconies, and your mother says *don't
tell your father that we have a phone*, you comply—

Unaware he already knows you have a phone, shrieking in the quiet
hall, and that he'll wait three years to tell you that he knows, three
years of feeding *Dad? It's me. Can you call me back?* into the avid
mouth of the red phone box down the road, on wet November
nights and piss-stink evenings in July—

So that when he asks you, again, *has your mother put a phone in yet?* and
you say *No*, again, your eyes easy in his gaze, because you've done this
lie so many times you swim right past it and you're fifteen, with far
more interesting fish to try—

29

Only this time he says, smiling like a shark, *I got the number from BT before she took it ex-directory*, and the weight of this one-thousand-day deception crashes through the fascinating waters of who is snogging who—

And all the passing mullet, skate and bream vanish in collective dorsal flexion, leaving you, lone flounder, in the saline shame of knowing that your lies can never be erased.

What is gout?

Gout is acid in the blood caused by too much meat and alcohol, and also vitriol, especially if exposure is continuous from early childhood, like rain, usually dripping into ears, like when your mother calls your father *a fucking mean shit, a pig, a bastard and a liar who only loves money, whose own parents couldn't love him*, like when your father tells you that your mother is not the woman you think she is, that she used to beat you with the flat back of your black, plastic Mason Pearson™ hairbrush before you can remember, or when you hear your mother talking on the phone *shouldn't laugh really, but honestly, one, two, three THUMP and then 'Mummy! I be's a fairy. Legs like tree trunks and the dress bursting at the seams <snort>* or when your father warns *You're so strident. No man will ever love you if you're so strident*, or your mother spits *you're just like your fucking father* which, when you think about it later, makes you *a fucking mean shit, a pig, a bastard and a liar who only loves money, whose own parents couldn't love you*. Over time, given the right conditions, the acid hardens into sharp crystals around certain joints, maybe a big toe, or an ankle, so that, eventually, every time you try to take a step, to move, it's as if you walked upon the points of razor blades, a thousand of them, like a mermaid who pays in pain for leaving the cold oceans of her people. And because your disability is hidden, in shoes, or socks, people cannot work out why you're always screaming, red in the face, cannot be touched on the sore parts. They mistake your pain for anger. You're best avoided, tricky, just not right. And when you have your own children, you prove it to the world. You're a wrong 'un. You deserved it, every bit of shit, and you've no right to judge. Acid runs in the family, in our veins.

David Rushmer

Intercourse

speak, then,
   of the disappeared
      of disappearance.

         a beginning
         swells
   this is your
         vast abyss
      of loss
      stripped of certainty

    in empty halls
      of language

     a moment of calm in white flowers

   words dilute on the breeze
detached from their brute
      energy
      creating
   a world without us.

    what makes you forget
      this memory

     the vanishing point
     and the tongue
a singular event

opening
the wind

forgotten
drafts
of light
becoming

                  intercourse

Rising in the Sap
(after Sappho)

I

    who is gone
    toward
        your gracious form
        on the
        tongue

waiting
    blasts of wind

that
sing us.

II

      carried you
        to garlands of
    delicate longing.

      we were absent.

no sound.

        moon
   and her light
barefoot
on the black earth

   broken chambers
      of stars
       poured upon
  the song

dripping gold weaving sleep.

III

     blowing
in this place

    to shine
    further sorrow

      breathed the sun
          to her ankles

         to become
         dawn again

    the brilliance new

   the heart
   they become.

IV

dream of
    blazing

   blossom
    delight
      in your soft hands
             flower
    shaped
   to listen.

V

    she spoke
of nowhere
with slender limbs

    wind falling
      burned with longing
      to touch the sky
         like roses
    wrapped in
      the memory of you.

VI

float
deep sound necklaces
    of wings
   under skin

eyes
greener than grass

moonform
on the earth

dripping winds
    burn me
    pour my thoughts

              wings
for a day.

Liam Ferney

February Release

I wait my turn for water behind a thirsty dog.
This is the way of things in Brisbane
where summer is elastic and the late afternoon
showers my legs and the world spins
like a dipping free kick in added time.

Running by the river the crab pots were empty,
the police boats full of teenagers as Sunday's
accumulation of adventure gone awry.
The echolalia of today, blueprints for next weekend.

The after party ache of red wine residue, beer bottles
baited with butts, last night's convenience cruelling
recycling's best intentions. And you skip out
quicker than a kiss, the film the marketing peeps
never figured out how to sell.

Leave

The world rehearses its catastrophes.
All of our Armageddons slurped
black aspirins on the chilly
patios of their morning afters.
You never remember to drink enough water.
The late June cold smears the sky.
Data bulges the hold, terror bites.
The ominous duff blimp spruiking
insurance hindenburgs over Milton;
last night's pedestrian blanketed
between a police car and an ambulance.
At some point we expect calamities,
like Lion's fans during Leppa's reign,

even if we are playing for sheep stations.
They leave a glass of gewürztraminer off
our bill and we leave without paying.

Milk Run to Canberra

Tonight she looked like rings.

Industry's captains clustered round the harbour.
Too close to wheels up
to listen to Satie, Canberra
half an hour downwind,
celeb news subtitles suffice –
Bingle's paparazzo bingle.

                    There are prophecies in fish guts
              we choose to ignore
but there's still time
for daylight savings disruption
before a day full of diabetes risk assessments
in a Parliament House corridor.

Waiting for your phone call
like a batsman whose heard the gossip
              wonders which way
Iverson's PNG perfected ping pong probe will break.

Your team might still win,
but that 17-ball duck
is the postscript of unfulfilled talent.
Fin.

Chloe Carnezi

"You must look upon Modern Greek as the impure dialect of a nation of peasants, just as you must look upon the modern Greeks as a nation of mongrel element & a rustic dialect of barbarous use beside the classic speech of the pure bred races."
—Virginia Woolf
Diary entry from her visit to Greece, 1906

Letter to Virginia Woolf

Helen exiled in Egypt.
Sand rubs her the wrong way, gets
Stuck in every
Fold and furrow of her
Flesh.

Body shameful,
Once the gift of a goddess, now
Body obscene in its thinness.

Breasts halved by a
Hunger mastectomy.

Still. She is Helen,
Helen-Hellene, who is not
Paris' to steal or
Elgin's to sack.

Mongrel element, yet
Helen of Greece,
Squeezing her handful of Earth.

Somewhere in Troy is a
Helen that *seems*, structured from
Vapour and rain.

This Helen of clouds wears a
Bonnet and corset and
Giggles with you over
Tea.

But remember: this Helen *is* not.

One day you will wake up alone.
She will be the Fog on your window in Sussex, and
There will be an Empty bonnet and dress, lying on your
Bedroom floor.

Aphrodite of Milos

Aphrodite of Milos
With stumps for arms.

Stumps like balloons filled with flour,
All tied up in
Anus-looking scars.

Helpless against the
Mildew of History and
Foreign Perverts.

If she woke up today
Would she be like the Hydra –
Sprout two arms on each side
For each one that was there axed?

With these new six limbs
And the spit of her narration
Of atrocities and

Ugliness,
The goddess of beauty would spin a web
And wrap up all men.

Or perhaps,
With legs and no arms,
Like a reverse mermaid,
She'd slither alongside us,
Through mud, cum, and centuries,

Until she took up begging at my doorstep.

Carmen Bugan

An old woman reading

One story ends and another opens on sunlit pages.
Though her arms seem burdened with the heavy book,
She is entirely inside the words, oblivious

To pain or being painted, her cloak the color
Of a red giant star, or the edges of planetary nebulae.
Rembrandt must have enjoyed their mutual silence,

As he poured earth from Siena with his hands
Over the granite table, mixing it with linseed oil
And his spatula, patiently waiting for her

To go into the chapters.
The Belgium heart stone looks grey-black;
You must grate the oil-soaked earth into granite

With its wide top: the top of the heart.
Some say she must be Hannah the Prophetess.
Then she must read about Time, and how

We are made of earth, for here
Is made of earth, oil, and stone. Breathing
Woman, image, story in painted earth.

★

The sun this morning shines through
Rembrandt's windows into his studio filled
With shells, heavy catalogues, philosophers' heads.

His old woman shall forever read in her frame
And we, of earth but not yet back into it,
Eat its other offerings: bright green wild pepper leaves

Sprinkled with roasted coconut and peanuts,
Lime, ginger, red onion, chili, dried shrimp,
And secret honey prepared by a chef from far away.

We taste the earthiness of his homeland
From his hands, which fold the wild pepper leaves
And set them into our mouths, gratefully.

His hands are old as hers, the skin under his chin
Sags like hers, but his house is fragrant. He touches us
The way she touches our minds--her shawl in embers,

And a sun that illuminates the book
Wider than her lap, opened to a space between
Chapters: out of timelessness and back.

Boy playing the cello

For Stefano

The chair he sits on is two hundred years old;
It modulates like the voice of his grandfather

Welcoming him to sit on his lap.
He straightens his back holding the cello

As if they're old friends. The two are about the same size.
This tree was chosen to make a different kind of music

From that of rain and wind that fell on its leaves,
Or from the dry woodpecker knock, the scratching

Claws of squirrels up and down its bark, branches and twigs,
The song of cardinals, robins and blue jays darting back and forth.

The boy holds the cello in his arms. His eyes are full of music,
Dreamy with notes about to happen, and the bow lies near

Like a promise of a journey. When he begins to play,
I think the heart of the tree gladdens in the dry,

Sunny house, giving into memories that long for summer
Thunderstorms, dawn choruses, in a low, echoing sound,

The wood, transformed, returns to its essence,
As the boy brings the marvelous into the house.

And now, the words

I struggle with the meaning of the word resurrection:
Go do your work, word, I say,
All the way back to your root. Then return to me
To stand by these children fished out of the luminous sea
So that I could see your face in
Horrified eyes, not saved, but filled with almost-life.

I used to be *resurgere,* rise again, the word says
Rising like the sound of the rain on a tin roof.
Remember, it says, dragging your refugee self
Out of the rumble of trains at Roma Termini,
And wanting to once again be free:
These children rise out of the sea like admonition.

I try to remember when the word arrived to me,
From whose mouth, or whose book I'd learned it,
And memory obeys: childhood Easter, Resurrection Mass
With a trail of candles in the night: *Invierea, Veniti sa luati lumina.*
Coming back to life, come take light. But these children
Fished out of the ancient Mediterranean:

This is my lifetime, resurrection, I say: children into the sea,
Swim away from the cataclysm of war, I see them
Pulled out of water, as if they are being lifted
Into the afterlife. Yet this is our life, is this what you mean

To me, in my lifetime, word? Shame burns
On the blue faces of children, bright like swords.

Put me next to the children, the word says, and I shout:
Resurrect Children. The glut of present opens:
There is no hell but here, no heaven but here,
The indicting eyes of children forced into the sea
Will never leave us, will no longer perish.
Here they are before me this Sunday morning,
Born on the horizon of nightmare, reaching with their tiny hands.

John Phillips

Possession

We think to possess a thing
by naming it, or so was thought

before words failed us. Or
we failed words. Nothing

possesses us now but words.
And words possess nothing

but what we say they do.

Exactly

As if there were
someone saying
these words
for someone

else to hear them
being said —
to make sense of
the act of saying,

the act of hearing —
or being here
doing either.
As if words could.

★ ★ ★

Tell me a story,
the words say

to no one there
listening. It's

themselves they
want to be told,

themselves they
want to hear.

The only thing
a story tells

is words happening
to be told.

from The Creation of Beauty
*for/from Mahmoud Darwish & Yehuda Amichai
& for John Berger*

I

Sometimes I want to
go back and forget

the letters of the alphabet.
I am tired of

my intractable hope,
tired like a room

in a hotel.
Behind my words,

dark as a moon,
the dove builds her nest

in an iron helmet. The soldiers
pitched their camp

in a faraway place and
she knows about

the resurrection of
the dead man

as he lies in her arms.

And I'll say:
I am not a citizen

and the prophets
died long ago.

One day I'll become
what I want,

not the peace
of a cease-fire.

V

Of all that has
ever happened,

we inherited
only our names.

Back then we
didn't know

what they were
teaching, but we

learned: Here or
there, our blood

will plant olive trees.

And because of the war

a young man
marries a girl

but they have no place
for their wedding night.

I open an iron door
over which is written:

This land is smaller
than the blood

of its offspring.

The almond tree
is in bloom.

What crime did I
commit to make you

destroy me?
Whenever I wake up

strange things
happen to me, yet

the author is not I.

VIII

Because of love
and because of

making love, I asked:
Is the impossible

far away? But at dusk,
in the thin rain,

a cafe, and you with
the newspaper, sitting.

If I could speak to
a woman on the road,

I would say: They did
what they had to do,

and drowned near
the shore.

And I want only
one thing, nothing more,

let me kiss you
one more time before

you no longer love it.
I have nothing to say

about the war, nothing —
and don't want a country.

Like dogs, drawn by
the smell, he said:

We will live, even if
life abandons us.

IX

A woman once
said to me: If you

wish to speak, you
must take action.

Everything comes true.

It's possible we might
find an answer.

In foreign countries
I rent hotel rooms

to desire, or to disappear.
As fate would have it,

sometimes she is naked
and not alone.

He said: I have reached
the end of the dream...

Words come to me now
like flies.

Everything begins to
resemble everything else.

It's as if I had died before now...
Don't promise me anything

and forgive me for
the things I didn't do.

XI

His words were
the simplest words:

I know that I know
how to kill.

Everything changes.
Everything.

If it were up to me
to bring back

the beginning,
I would.

Sometimes they celebrate,

punctuating time
with the same

ancient war machine.
Whenever I think

about the woman
and the garden

I want only to return.
At night I walked again

along the row of
empty willows — no one

behind me; no one
ahead.

But what's the meaning
of this thing?

We talked a great deal
about death.

The soldiers in the grave
say: You, up there.

What do you want?

Rachael Clyne

Bedtime

When it's dark the man behind the wardrobe in the corner gloops like hot marmite I try to ignore him then say in my loudest voice MY DADDY'S A POLICEMAN AND HE'S IN THE NEXT ROOM except he's not and he's deaf. When it's dark the branch-fingers scratch to get in and the chimney moans but I know it's the really-dark 'cause I can't hear the TV and there's only me. Just when I'm nearly asleep they start yelling through the wall behind my head YOU BULLY ... DON'T YOU YELL AT ME ... BASTARD! I put my fingers in my ears and it stops. Just when I'm nearly asleep they start up again. But now I have my Koshy cat he sleeps with me. Now I have Koshy I pretend we fly through the really-dark on a broom and come back when the shouting's stopped and go to sleep.

Apocalypse Shoes

Whatever past-life, barefoot memory haunts her—she must have stout shoes for Armageddon. She bought buffalo shoes in California. They were her insurance. Come the collapse, she'd work the land. Greased with dubbin, her thick-skinned buddies should last a lifetime. Alas they fell along the urban-fashionista wayside, in favour of Terry de Haviland scarlet leather, tarty straps. Dystopian fears have returned to adorn her shoe-rack. They'll house her feet, help her flee the neo-Nazi knock on the door. With Yaktrax attached, she can escape on ice. She has enough pairs to see her through a post-petroleum Arctic melt. When Hinkley Point collapses, she'll stride across the Levels, sack of brown rice on her back, windup torch in her hand.

The Owls Are Not What They Seem

They appear indifferent, but fix me
with slow blinks, ready to stealth-bomb,
spit me out in neat pellets.

A mirror switches the left-right of my face
an oasis of friendship that sustained me
evaporates into desert.

I grow vague with years
much of what I used to care about
no longer holds interest.

Those beliefs in social progress,
revolution—just a heap of old clothes
to take to the charity shop.

I adjust to the endless cycles of order
and mayhem. Each generation finds
the previous one lacking, now it's my turn

to be redundant as a telephone box.
But the hardest rock contains seabed
a leaf can conceal an infinite outline

and our stardust bodies
will continue to re-form. What remains
is as wondrous as a kingfisher.

The title is a quote from the TV series, Twin Peaks.

Susie Campbell

Settling with my madness

Naked, except for her turquoise skin. From each pierced nipple swings a silver charm—a camel with a ruby mouth—a Babel tower an inch high. She begins the dance. Cameras zoom in as she struts with pointed toes, somersaults with squirrel grace and lands with a flick of her wrists.

Handwritten labels peel from clear glass: medicine bottles crammed full of bitter sherbets in the old sweet factory; children's marbles for stoppers—striped *aggies*—blind-white *milkies*—a brutal *blood-alley*. I hide her in the attic. Down in the street, straw effigies grin and swagger, whistling through sewn lips: *help us, we need purges, syrup of figs and liquorice twists.*

.   .   .

They drag the river again. A kayaker sucked from his canoe grows gigantic—as the drowned always do—and fills the river with his trailing arms and slackened lips. Even the rubber-suited divers know the water gives back its bodies only when it is done, deposits them hollow and laced together with weed. They visit me—the drowned—leave footprints on my doorstep, a smear of green slime on my china; this paper, draped with nettles and long purples, lying wet on the floor.

On the earth and under the earth

i.

hollow | excavate | buried | echo | beneath | surface | voices |
underside | deep

ii.

The house is haunted: its ghosts, stitched down in *millefleur* tapestries,
sprout daisies from broken cheeks to weave a carpet for sharp *licorne*
hooves; a grace pleasing in the dead. The virgin tilts her bleached
pelvis shocking the tourists: the dead are not supposed to dance. But
nothing is as it seems. Not the gouts of light, scarlet and royal blue,
spilt on the floor, nor the stain rising up the walls. But we have not
come to it yet.

Beneath the flagstones wedged over bone, something yawns and
gawps. Threatens to unstring stories and roll their teeth like yellow
marbles.

iii.

As the abyss makes angels question.

What difference does this great hollow make? How do these ruins,
les thermes, release my architecture, undo its poles?

If not double, incompatible in its parts.

Or if single, a grace-note, a handful of salt thrown—haphazard—over
one shoulder.

*(The Musée de Cluny in Paris houses the 'La Dame à la licorne' tapestries, whose meanings
remain uncertain. The house was built over the remnants of ancient Roman baths.)*

Shorn

(with lines from Niall Campbell's Fleece*)*

Venice: university of watermark and untruth. Our cowled flight here; this waking under cover of golden flesh. Our tongues, once tied in vows to others, now loosen in heroic lies. Our love fattens on legend.

Beneath my neck a garland of crushed lilies. Your curled hand kneads your throat: tight with dream, a butcher's garrote. A fret of light, forged in the city's red shambles, honeycombs our knitted limbs, *leavening the gold from the pale underskin.* Your waking face turns away. It is done. The shining wool is cut, *head right down to the knife line … dub-dub of the heart.* Blade blunts, the naked animal is clumsily dispatched.

Without gold, the water turns black. Its cold canals rinse myth from lies. Tufts of greasy wool slip from our fingers as the heavy body rolls, leaves its reddish stain on the tide.

Teenage werewolf syndrome

Nowhere to sit among the spots of mould freckling the slats, nowhere to stand in the ferment of spilt talcum. Our sweat-stained shorts and yeasty socks twine on the floor; air curdles in the C of a forbidden word yipped backwards and forwards as the locker-room door swings shut. Penned in with our pungent steam, little toadstools turn sticky in the cracks. We raise the temperature, blister paint off walls; bubble syrup from the boards.

.   .   .

Nowhere to hide from scoops of hip and belly laid bare, bare underarm flesh pimpled and nicked. Just me born with it. Lanugo. Soft fuzz meant to rub off, not thicken to this thick auburn pelt. Nowhere to hide its bristling dorsal tuft. I bare my teeth, slink from the shower, nowhere to chase or nip or tussle. I squat and piss on the mat, hot and acid-yellow.

(Hypertrichosis, aka Werewolf Syndrome, is the abnormal growth of body hair.)

Claire Potter

The Salamander

My salamander slid into the coals of the kitchen where I had burnt
your dinner and called it

not my day, but my indifference to being a mother. Being
an entity that at any other time I would have called my salamander
sulking in the coals, but this indifference was cold, no eyes at all

It was something dark like a joint of imperfect heart, a
salamander cloven in the coals.

The Unicorn

The polar bear takes me to an Alaskan village. The bear is treading through wasteland, its white coat ruddied and dieselled, eyes wayward, vision dislodged, not forward but sideways and insular. I wince at the photograph of the bear, think of a student who pushed a block of melting ice through the grainy streets of London, his own traces of foreignness slipping away. I'd like to talk more about his film, but I'm stuck with the polar bear and a graph of climate change that layers science over the Arctic. There's scant left to measure, but I can't leave the Arctic, it's shrinking around me, cloaking me in disappearance, in leaving. The polar bear looks out of place in the village, he is iceless, snouting for food, lodged in a bone pile of whale. I follow him there into the carcasses, into bins scavenging, hissed at to leave, fur quiffed red in the patrol car's light, frightening locals like a lone wolf honing in for leftovers whilst we make trips to visit the Arctic Circle and observe what's left of polar bears. I smell rust and diesel in the photo, see the cogs and wires, the black grease of tyres, every tangle of steel and plastic. The bear is small in comparison with the structure of rubbish. I want to get out of Alaska, I can't be here anymore, I'm reading the newspaper because it's showing me an Alaska I've never visited before. Words hold pitch perfect, but questions creep in, if this is not a polar bear, then what is it? I'm hot under my collar sitting on the ice, I'm watching the bear loop apace around a pile of rubbish as though my being in the Arctic is an equation. I sympathise with the bear, I'm not looking at what I'm doing, I'm wiping fingerprints over his ears and jaw, his polar coat is the colour of newsprint, he's a Frankenstein bear we've built from sawdust and now refuse to talk to.

Ladder of Parole

If my mistake
of calling you
Cubist amongst men
is to be believed
it is because
my old love
I wanted to see you
again, see a tweed
cuff or a fraction
of cerulean eye
but I'm aphasic
in the way a cat's cry
melts into the wind————————
I only glimpse you
in pieces
you're gossamer
down the street
catgut wide
hived in
hopscotch through
the cemetery crowd, but
forgive this
I'm just bottling separation
for a few
moments more
tears of annual zest
rising
like stalagmites
warning
against the mistake
of thinking
I'll see a whisker
of you again
———————————and
not simply
again and again and again.

Cadenza

} My Croatian grandmother   made me
a percentage mad   she learnt English
from labels   on tins   at the supermarket
where she pushed a trolley   up
down   buying variations
of the same dish
that didn't   require perfect reading
until a sentence   could be strung
like close your mouth   there's only time
to say something   less like
I'm a mother   I've five kids   I lost two
on a dirt floor over a mat bed   I over-
lock wedding dresses for middle class ladies
What's that, my name?   Anna   Anne   Annie
let me get you something   to eat
some thing   are you hungry   let me cook
for all this crying   put in here flour   a cup
now half a pint of milk   three eggs crack here   for you
whisk it   for me then   soften butter   sugar
cinnamon lemonade   two cups of sultanas
set the timer   and finished   you'll feel better
read me the label   it says   tell me what it says
I don't know where am I   am I   what   no   what
nothing   go   take me some rosemary from the back
of the garden   give your grandfather   a glass of water
and his jar of musk lollies   here's the tray   go on   *dobro*
she kisses and ushers me out   into the garden
where Nonno is sitting on the low brick wall
blended in runner beans   and the jurassic sprawl
of dark zucchini leaves whose flowers spill
and pull sunshine   into their long   yellow heads
——————ragged vines swarm underfoot   Nonno's eyes
are double egg-timers   measuring the weeds   telling Baka
when the vegetables are ripe enough   to be brought inside {

*Baka is Croatian for Grandma

61

Lucy Hamilton

from Dissecting the Family

Gold Leaf Boy

I cut a clean line down the centre of his head & face
He's split into two hemispheres and it's for me to decipher

the logical left eye & the creative right | for me to choose
Next the leaf | not hammered into a sheet of 22 karat

Picked from a sycamore by the Cam and bleeding red
green & yellow on my trestle | The leaf curls & crinkles

as I splice it to his right face | gold against 50s Kodak hair
anthracnose spots & veins juxtaposed with boy-fresh skin

broken tooth & freckles | The textured shape of the leaf
conjours & echoes fruit & pulse | food & fluid & function

foreshadows an organ he will lose to tumour | But now
framed under the light of my lamp | the boy's leaf-face

my highlights in his hair and the flexible stalk overhanging
the top of his head | there's a hint of cherub | golden apple

Siblings & Geranium

Yes, like people, art objects change and do not change
—Anthony Rudolf

As I fix the frame pegs and stand back to view it's not
the incongruity of faces conjoined at their centres like found

middle-ground in difference or dispute | I know the story
the tomboy & the bookworm | one remains and one's departed

The school dresses are vague in memory but vivid in the album
And it's not even the fresh geranium clipped to the bookworm's

curly dark hair in amends for the lipstick that fails or the fact
that one petal folding as another falls is mildly disturbing | No

but since J said that the pictures *spook* him I can't view them
as I did before | Like the siblings they have changed/not

changed and I the maker/viewer oscillate between perspectives
like the ancients when arranging geraniums for solar spells

Viewer | Viewed

The face arrests me as I slide its left side partially
under its right | synchronising the crown of the head

and swept back hair until what's left of the left is blank
its listening ear slightly raised and prominent as if to

highlight a shrewd & fine-tuned instrument | Her beauty
vibrates undiminished between the single eye & ear

as I paste her onto the copied pre-War paperback page
frame her with scraps of blue like an arch or window

and glue the cut out phrase *plus tôt elle avait paru désolée*
Now as I stand back to view her one eye viewing me

the paradox of half-truth & perfection catches me out
and sends me back to the text to discover that *elle*

refers to *cette église* and can't be attached to my mother
I restore the words | amused by her eye's sharp insight

The Bust [III]

In the final years of my mother's life we always greeted the Bust
'Lalla Maghnia' as we passed her by the stairs | Now as I slide

her photographed head onto an image of my sister's dress
I balk at an imagined clash of settings | the western restaurant

brash against the Maghreb where Lalla Maghnia was Raj es Salin
The Bust's sweet face has such an air of meditation & nostalgia

I juxtapose the photo with a picture of a goat-filled Argan tree
envisaging furls of morning dung-smoke | aromas of baking bread

as the village stirs | the women chatting & teasing | the scene
a strange mix of 18th century Algeria with my trip to Morocco

The sky's deep blue reflects on Lalla's head-dress and on the turban
worn by a male figure who stands observing under the branches

And now it's not the visual incongruity that jars but the memory
of a goatherd's joy as his small brown hands danced on my iPad

Ho Cheung Lee

Wrapping Paper

Uncle's body found.
For how long he'd been lying
next to his bed we don't know,
the doctor didn't say. His neighbours
smelled him and made the call.

This afternoon, his sister, my mother-in-law,
waited at the mortuary's reception for
the large orange door to slide.
Her mind a vacuum for three minutes
nine seconds.
The tanned butcher man understood her difficulty.

Just stay right there, yes,
just stay where you are.
Just a glance will do. Yes.
That's him alright? Good.

And is his name correct?

Her muted vomit followed
her frustration that spilled out
from the top of her dark glasses.
The stink was agonizing—
it carried his face
and story of his last hours
stabbing through her shut eyelids.
It hummed.

On the way to the crematorium,
the driving lady in purple spoke not a word.
Alan Tam's duet with Teresa Carpio
muffled the passengers with

the oldies, lingering as if we
played them within our skulls.

The dangling fragrance bag in its
kimono danced to the voices as I
tore open the white packet
for the coin and the candy.

The wrapping paper's red,
rustling.
As I was about to dump it into
the cup-holder at my arm rest,
I found three pieces already
filling the unwanted hollow.
All emaciated, lifeless, forgotten.

The Temple Man

18:26.
The depressive sun still cast two
towering shadows in front of the
misty outlines, inching towards
me like two hollowed figures
surfaced from the dried, barren earth.
The visitation was punctual and silent.
They smelled like roots as they passed by,
liquefying into the smoke-drowned room.
Their words did not actually leave the aura that
draped their emptied bodies.
The boy turned his head once, his eyes
sparkled like dark pearls which
reminded me of myself waiting—
waiting to be taken at his yard sale. The day
he last climbed down from our old bed
where I lay flat to dream that my

bare chest still felt his left arm
from his remaining scent. The bedding
stained like blossoms. I heard the last
seagull stirring the gods behind me.

I hear the gods behind me every time
before the temple gates close.

five feet away

i.m. Mrs Lau Choy Yim Ling (1968-2015)

Seventh month of the moon calendar

A friend called and asked me to confirm
your husband's message

It was a bad joke

The boy was excused before
you left the bed and the six tubes
running through the emaciated body
like glass tentacles draining from a decaying prey

In your night gown you don't sleep

The aged woman burning paper offerings
in the street veiled by the mellifluous mist
Street lamp flickered, children questioned, ashes
carried away

I try to look for you and the rest
roaming around my car as it halts
The cracks and stains and wounds
on the walls need much imagination

Ventilation humming deep
A suppressed moan

I can't help scrolling backwards in time
Our last conversation never started

Your makeup
This final selfie

(I really wasn't lying
You are beautiful)

I stroke your frozen face and convince myself
that your lips curl

You are the song about stars
the verve in your disconnected words
the composure
      his eyes

Marius told me about the grasshopper
on the front screen of the car this morning

I see no moth but a flattened red-whiskered bulbul
five feet away

Martin Anderson

Under Jiu-yi Shan

"I now state my terms to the crocodiles. I set them a limit of three days to take their ugly selves south to the sea ... Do not repent when it is too late!"
—Han Yu, *Address to the Crocodiles of Chaozhou*

I

By the east lake the wind blows hard.
Over reed marsh, mud flat and shallow.
Tundra swan, stork and crane already
have landed. Out of that far barbarian
heaven where snow falls and falls without
stopping. Where, leaving, day after day they heard
nothing but the sound of wind through passes,
across ice-locked rivers, sweeping
the slightest hint of warmth before it.
At the lake edge I stand. Listening. Sedge, crisp
with frost, under my feet crunches. Wondering
at how winter has arrived so early.

II

On Great Marsh of Cloud Dream, alone,
I compose verses, to which no one will listen.
The court of Chu puff themselves up,
parade around, bristle. Idle and poisonous
chatter is all they engage in: a quagmire
of lies, vilifications and distortions.
They would, if they had to,
fill a bag of flowers with excrement
and proclaim that it smells fragrant.
They'd rather, I am sure, that I obliged
by falling into a river full of crocodiles

than ever reappearing amongst them. On
Great Marsh of Cloud Dream I chant
and the birds accompany me, migrants
from far lands, in a music of impending chaos.

III

Mist rolls in over muddy flag filled bottoms.
A rufous sandstone cloud erupts
from the lake's bed, when the foot's
thrust in it. A darkening pandemonium.
Beside me sweet caneflower-
silvergrass leans and shivers. Cold
October air. Wisps linger and curl
over long silt-spits that glisten half submerged.
From creek-head to creek-head the sound
of the rites. Drumming. Drumming.
Drumming. Unabated. Each nubile waist
encircled by an arm. Dancing and
pursuing in the flux and twist of air and
water the whirlwind and the storm. To ease
the dried out heart. To atone. Old
crocodile skin, stretched under the
hand, whose broken lachrymose fate
is conjured and elucidated in your note?

IV

Eaten under the shade of
Jiu-yi Shan, in the dark water
close to Burned Field Village.
At the placid, lapping margin.
So completely devoured, no sign
of them remaining. In each loose-reign
prefecture I ride through, carts loaded.
Families adrift on the roads. Sour

smelling, brackish the taste of a life
lived under Jiu-yi Shan. Far out
the sound of a storm brews over the water.
Muffled, intermittent rumbling.
I listen. Leaves of the orchid
tremble. Fleabane glimmers at the water's
edge, damp from a low cloud that hangs
heavily above it. In the air, scent
of cassia. Over the south running channels.
I point my horse's head toward them.
With a stumble, and a sigh, we follow.

V

Within a charred circle of sourgrass
ash of incense and powdered bone.
Impress of makeshift shrine, dismantled.
Cloud black over vastness of water sky all
the way back to Ying. The damp wind spawns
sinister phantoms that writhe and twist
their way into the heart, when one is
not looking. Sinuous as guts of sacrifice
spread out and interpreted. But who
is the one who yields the life, and the
one who takes it? The sanctimonious cant
of those who thrive, courtiers covetous
of their own comfort and future, only drives the
knife deeper. I came upon this bloodstained
spot at evening, my horse exhausted
my stomach cramped with hunger, long after
the rites had ended. Behind me
from the scattered bivouacs of those from
Chu who'd fled, rather than remain to see
the coming disaster, smoke was rising.

VI

The Imperial Inquisitors of Chin, a country
of wolves and tigers, sit in their gold
plated palanquins and dispense
injustice. Connoisseurs of terror their fingers whiten
often. No room for treatises on music,
philosophy or history in the Imperial
Archive. They burn them. And no need
to bury your head in the sand—they
will, if you write or read such nonsense,
do it for you. Or get someone else to:
there's never any shortage of hoodlums
among us. Each night paranoia stalks their
bedchambers. Informers in every household.
When the wind blows south, over the
Han River, it is full of black dust.
Cities, townships and villages. Burning.
Slowly, it filters down upon us.

VII

Waste of protectorates, of vassals.
North of the Han River. A cold wind
cracks the faces, tears the banners of
Chin armies. But still they move south
ward devouring, like a silk worm, leaf
upon leaf. Massing on our borders.
Pretending it is we who are threatening
theirs. What can't be expropriated
by force they expropriate by trickery and
deception. Chin Shih Huang-ti, face of a
jackal breast of bird of prey, has torn off
the cankered flesh of our court, bit by bit.
Gnawed through its heart. So easy to destroy
such credulous self-flattering fops
trading gold and precious stones for enslavement.

Jin Shang, Cheng Hsiu, Tzu Lan. May
you consume what you have harvested.

VIII

All the fragrant leaves have withered.
Orchid, sun-apple, white rumex, cart-halting
flower, sweet spirit grass. Fleabane bends
back in the wind. Over the muddy bottom
under Jiu-yi Shan my reflection wavers.
Words, like stones, sink. On the air strange accents.
From far prefectures northward. From a
government geared for war, not peace: women tilling
fields, men away expanding borders. Outlaws
in the forests and the marshes. I raise my head.
A faint drumming over the dark waves. The wind
blows hard. Cold hands lift cold water to
parched lips. White as thistledown my breath.
Suddenly all the birds are leaving.

Chu Yuan was a high ranking minister in the State of Chu during the fourth and
third century BCE. Because of court rivalries ("Day and night they curse and vilify
me.") and of his hostility to the growing power of the State of Chin, a proto-
fascist Legalist state, he was exiled south to a non-Sinitic culture and region, present
day Hunan, where he traversed ceaselessly the vast undrained swamps and wetlands
around the Dongting lakes. His famous long poem *Li Sao* (Encountering Sorrow)
was pro-foundly influenced by the shamanistic songs and lore of the region. His
death by his own hand in the Miluo River is commemorated, each fifth day of the
fifth month of the traditional lunisolar calendar, by the dragon boat festival. The
dragon on the boat prow is a motif which derives from the crocodile. *Under Jiu-yi
Shan* (Nine Doubt Mountain, a site in southern Hunan sacred as the burial place of
Shun one of the most revered rulers of antiquity noted for his moral stature) embeds
various lines from *Li Sao* and observations on Chu Yuan by Su-ma Ch'ien the Great
Recorder of the first century BCE.

Eiffel Gao

情有独钟 / Singular Amour

My thoughts about you are as clammy and raw
as the fume beneath the shoulder seam
of your summer shirt.
My hatred of you fizzes through and spoils
every phrase that possesses your name.
Love poems became mine fields;
Chinese egressed;
Another language from another country upholstered me.

You whisked away my eighteen-year-old pride
solved my feelings with a dimple
and strafed my best dreams.
How dare you, still,
call me by that sobriquet
whose sounds make young bracken curl.

Not a word came between us
during that last thundershower in Ningbo
when we stood before high French windows
watching the glacial skyscrapers dissolve into pearl-grey.
I was gazing down into the rotundity of human toil
when suddenly the outer world dimmed much further
and from the craquelure reflection I saw you gazing into me.

General Zhang After the Battle of Chibi

"If Sky had feelings, Sky would age too." —Li He (Tang)

With jade-white fingers holding an ebony brush,
calligraphy and shadows swinging upon the cicada paper
like a crane sliding across a lake alongside its reflection,
I imagine you.

Last night poets sang with the Yangtze River,
weaving wind into music and pouring poetry into wine.
"This earth and this dome are ours," I laughed.
You were lying on your back with the moonlight, and simply said:
"But after we're gone, whose will they become?"

Today the Northern invaders came clad in steel.
Heads rolled between hoofs like stray dogs.
My troop was whittled down, my brothers.
A curving sword pierced through my body.
I stand like this, for it will not let me fall.

'Sky, let him return to me.' You would pray.
Go find my bones ossified in the Great Wall
the golden tip of my sword in a cloisonné
and my name scattered in the chronicles.

Dynasties have come and gone in a wink.

Do you see, as I do, that summer day?
Down like a waterfall, your black hair
pricked me like the beard of wheat.
Suddenly, under the sunlight
coming through the slit of the tent,
a lock of your hair shined silver:
I stopped and held it in my hand—
I thought it was white already—
in my shadow it was black again.

I feel the dust of fluttering crows.
The battle is won; the frontier holds;
and all is spilt. Take me in,
I command these debased corpse-followers,
take me to see once again
the breathing rivers
the endless hills
the land where vast beauty reclines unchecked—
This land—my immemorial country—
shall be with you always.
Oh, my ultimate relief.

A Hundred Ways of Torture

> Fang Xiao Ru came from Ninghai, Ningbo: a prodigy since
> youth and an upright official in the Ming dynasty. We have a
> temple for him on a quiet hill.

<<< By The Nine Clans Exterminations

The third Ming emperor, a usurper,
looked over the court and wondered
who was loyal:
the kneeling officials between vermilion pillars,
like red and blue dumplings in a lacquered box,
dared not breathe.

Fang Xiao Ru was not in court.
The Emperor ordered Fang to come
to write an imperial verdict
to convince the people
that the country was in the right hands.

In white mourning dress Fang came, and his wails
would have felled the carved dragon on the golden glazed roof.

The brush he flung away stained the white jade stairs.
The king threatened to kill Fang's nine clans.
Fang said: 'Kill ten and still I will not write for you.'
So the king did.

Over 800 people; like pulling up an enormous vine of tomatoes.
'Fang' became an extinct surname in our town
for more than a century.

<<< By 3600 Scrapes from 3600 Knives

Fang himself, it's said, was honoured
with the most scrupulous method of torture.

The first day, a few hundred scrapes;
each from a unique knife
designed to tender a particular pound of flesh.
And then some porridge before tomorrow.
The second day, he lost his voice.
The third day, his flesh began to stink.
The executor had to pause longer
so that Fang would not pass too soon.

How many days now?
He had lost count.
How much more left?
For a time he feared he might not die.

But when the emperor came around
in an amber sedan pavilion
and Fang heard the silver-toned performers sing—
Flitting willow catkins; bouquets; a Maytime sun—

He breathed this last thought.
How very beautiful.

<<< By Unresolved Love

During her first week abroad,
an unacquainted woman on a podium pointed at her
as a representative of Asian specialists in plagiarism.

One of her recurring nightmares:
they disregarded her with benevolent silence, when, unconsciously,
she replied in her native tongue.

Once she thought that the terracotta warriors
accompanying the First Qin Emperor to the grave
were really devoted real people,
coated with a layer of clay and then baked in a kiln,
smiling throughout
to be entombed and figured under perpetual awe.

<<< By the Course of History

Seligman's oriental collection made famous
the illustrated booklet enumerating methods of torture.
You've been wrong to think I know them better.

The emperor who tortured Fang Xiao Ru to death founded the
        Forbidden City.
The Old Summer Palace by the later emperors was uprooted in one fall
and set on fire for three days and three nights; more than 300 burnt alive.

Confucius said, *what you do not want yourself,*
Do not impose it on others.
I think he meant, when we have a choice.

Time collects our loyalties
as a dam collects leaves in a rainy season.

Naka Tarō

translated by Nihei Chikako & Andrew Houwen

Décalcomanie II

shi (poem)   is the needle's gleam spreading on the marble
me (eye)   is the magnet on which its light converges

shi (death)   is the invisible sap climbing up the tree
me (bud)   is the thorn it feeds pricking the outside world

★

shi (poem)   is the shadow of the soaring bird
me (eye)   is the rifle bullet following in its tracks

shi (death)   is the moth's disturbance circling the night's crown
me (bud)   is the flame subsiding on the candlestick

★

shi (poem)   is the black rose
me (eye)   is the trembling antenna

shi (death)   is the sea-bed's tangled algae
me (bud)   is the slicing blade

★

shi and *shi*   are the ciphers
me and *me*   are the decipherers

shi and *shi*   are the pollen
me and *me*   are the carriers

Landscape with Fishbones

climbing up the glass spiral staircase
a decrepit beast   all its hair gone
the only one left behind   a desert stretches
in front of the blind being's eyes
here and there huge things like fishbones protrude
drawing the eye like a paper kite   the desiccated image of a god

in the clear ether of the sky
hira hira hira hira
endlessly fluttering down like banknotes
like millions of pages   torn to pieces
the sublimated anguish and the cries
of a people that had once destroyed itself
by the well into which they sank
not even a dream of the world's beginning
nor even a shadow of reincarnation remain

in the far distance
a half-transparent sun like a broken watch
half-buried in the sand

Romanesque

there is not much time left
everything is up in the air
nothing to be done   anything goes
Albrecht van der Qualen
arriving at an unknown station on an evening thick with fog
in an unknown town's   wet gas-lit street
passing through an old twin-towered gate
crossing an iron bridge over a river splitting into three
always turning left wherever he went
Albrecht van der Qualen
suddenly he reached the end of the town and then

rang the bell of a door with a rooms to let sign and then
what happened every night in those rented rooms?
talking with nightmares?   a game of chess with the dead?
making love with alluring naked women who cried and cried?
Albrecht van der Qualen
at the heart of the silently dancing candle-flame
there is not much time left
everything is up in the air

*Albrecht van der Qualen is a character in a work by Thomas Mann [author's note]

July

1

the Kannon temple bell distantly echoes
the burning of the chaff   scorches the night sky of memory
fetching the sea water   at Gion Yamakasa festival

2

the rain's harp sweeps past in *allegro*
irises   peonies   rhododendrons too   swept past
from a green wound a drop drips *andante*

3

rotting grass gives birth to fireflies
a lily morphs into a butterfly
in the sky swim countless silver fish

4

one morning white waves come crashing into the mind
the endless traveller   alone
walks through beautiful southern streets

5

amid the rubble water bursts from pipes
tears are burnt and parched
darkly bright   noon

6

the author of *Spinning Gears* drank Veronal
on an innocent young day   for the first time
I felt the terror of life

Osip Mandelstam

translated by Alistair Noon

Four Poems

I marvel at the kids and snow,
and at the light some more—
no faithful servant but a road,
this smile that no one's forged.

December 1936–1938 (?)

Goldfinch friend, when I tilt my head
we see the world like twins.
But is the spiky sky – think seed –
as cruel in your pupil this winter?

Yellow and black, your tail like a boat,
below your beak you blush.
Did you know that you're so goldfinch,
the goldfinch kind this much?

Black and yellow, red and white.
The air gone into that crown!
He keeps his eyes peeled either side—
then stops—and off he's flown.

9–27 December 1936

Today is kind of yellow-gobbed,
I can't say why. The gates
to the sea pierce anchors and fog
to fix me with their gaze.

Silent warships pace and pace,
the water loses its dyes,
and each canal's a pencil case,
blacker beneath the ice.

9–28 December 1936

The goldfinch goes into shudders
in its airy muffin, all cardiovital,
professor in its fine black cap, then spite
shakes pepper on its gown all of a sudden.

The cage's one hundred knitting needles
and the slat accuse it, the perch concurs.
And inside-out is all the earth:
a Salamanca of trees indeed
for wise, disobedient birds.

December 1936

Philippe Jaccottet

translated by Ian Brinton

Insight

Look at the children running in full cry
through thick grass of the school playground.

Mid-morning September light showers down
in a cool fall and unmoving tall trees
shelter them from the giant anvil
casting off starry sparks
in the beyond.

*

Must such a timid and shivering soul
walk non-stop across this glacier,
solitary and unshod, unable to piece together
a prayer from infancy,
being chastised for its coldness by the cold?

*

Such little knowledge gained after
such a wealth of years,
faltering heart?

Not even a penny to tip
the ferryman when he comes to knock?

I have merely put aside grass and running water,
not weighting myself down—
so his boat can ride the stream.

*

The mirror is round like the mouth
of a child incapable of deception.
She approaches; wrapped in a blue
dressing-gown showing
signs of wear.

Before long, hair settles to the colour
of ash in time's slow-burning fire.

Her shadow still hardens
in the early morning light.

*

On the far side of a window, the whitewashed frame
of which repels both flies and ghosts,
the hoar-frost head of an old man bows
above a letter or just the local news.
Darkening ivy creeps against the wall.

May whitewash and ivy protect him from dawn breeze,
long nights and that darkness without end.

*

Raked light on water gives below the surface
a shape of trees. However hard I peer
I cannot catch a glimpse of this weaver
whose hands one would love to touch.

As loom and cloth and room all fade
one should surely find
footprints planted in damp ground...

*

For a moment we rest still within a cocoon of light.

As that unravels (with patience or in haste)
can we not, as peacocks through the night,
jet out wings decked in eyes
to carry us through the darkness and the cold?

*

Sight into these things and more
(despite a trembling hand and knocking heart)
beneath this same sky:
gleaming garden squash, eggs laid by sun,
violet flowers hinting of old age.

If this glimmer of summer's end
dazzles with the shadow of yet more to come,
I should scarcely find myself
in less surprise.

Virgil

translated by David Hadbawnik

from Aeneid, Book VIII

WAR!

      WAR!

            WAR!

    booming from every speaker:

                WAR!

    everyone's in a tizzy:

WAR!

    car horns honking

    guns firing

      straight up in the air:

        WAR!

I pledge allegiance

    to the flag

        WAR!

        for which it stands

    one nation

kids

      worked up into

            patriotic frenzy

emissary to Diomede:

    "Hey

    Aeneas and his weak-assed gods
    have infested Latium
    he's calling himself a king
    and his name rings out
    on every corner
    god knows if we don't
    nip this thing in the bud
    what he'll do (if he's lucky
    in battle), well, I don't need
    to spell it out for you."

So it goes in Latium—

    Brave Prince Aeneas, meanwhile
            fluctuates
    his soul beat thin as a leaf
            twisting
    this way and that
    catching the moonlight and tossing it
            high on the wall
    like a question or a prayer

    while everyone else sleeps
    Aeneas lies by the river
    heart torn by murmurs of war

    the river god himself rises up
    from the Tiber

covered in moss, hair tied back in a reedy knot
and whispers these words:

"You
        godseed
                prince
among men
        don't shrink from
seizing this,
        your new home.
The deep bruise
of divine anger
has gone down,
nothing can stop you now.
            Don't believe me?
Nearby there's a huge sow
that's just delivered 30 white piglets
eagerly suckling away
a sure sign that 30 years on your son
will found a great white city:
        ALBA
Still don't buy it? There's more:
Up the road a ways
are some real tough bastards:
the Arcadians, a breed
sprung from Pallas, they're always brawling
with the Latins,
go make peace with them
I'll lead you there myself,
all you have to do is paddle
—Oh, say a prayer to Juno,
make it good, calm down
the last of her womanly anger.
And don't forget me
        when you win—I'm the Tiber,
        heaven's favorite stream."

. . .

It just so happens King Evander's out with his son, Pallas
        paying homage to Hercules
        (the youths and politicians on hand
        are a "who's who" of the kingdom,
        such as it is), when they see the boats
        sliding through the woods—freaked out,
        everyone abandons the bloody meat
        smoking on altars and PALLAS
        yells from a long ways off:

        "Who
                the fuck
                        are you?
        What are you doing here?
        Are you lot looking for trouble,
                or what?"

Father Aeneas, literally holding an olive branch, shouts back:

        "We're Trojans!
        We're here to fight the Latins (they started it!)
        and we want to talk to Evander,
        see if he's on our side."

Trojans? Pallas can't believe
        this blast from the past.

"Goddamn. Well, whoever you are,
        come on down. I'll take you into our house myself
        and introduce you to dad."

And there on the shore they hug like old friends.

Aeneas to Evander:
        "Hello, great king! Or should I say—cousin!
        That's why I'm not scared even though
        you're Greek and we Trojan, fucked
        by your gods—divine seed runs

in both our bloodlines, so I come to you
as no artful dodger but a brother-in-arms
with hat in hand. These bastards attacking us
are wild at heart, give them an inch
they'll take the sky and swarm
            every last shoreline."

Evander

        looking Aeneas up and down
        this whole time, taking in
        his face, eyes, the shape
        of his body, says

        "Damn
                if you're not the spitting image
        of your father, Anchises!
        Many years ago we met and exchanged
        kisses and greetings and gifts.
        I burned to befriend him,
        him, noble above all Priam's boys.
        He gave me a golden scarf, gold spurs
        (now worn by my son, Pallas)
        and a wonderful Lycian gun.
                SO:
        Here's the helping hand you seek,
        and I won't let you leave without
        fresh men and supplies.

In the meantime,

        you've caught us in the midst of our annual party—
        so why not join in the fun and get a head start
        on local customs?
                Sit! Sit! I insist," he says, and orders a round
        of drinks for the boys and for Aeneas—
                "Come, come!"
        —the best seat in the house,
                a huge recliner cushioned with lion's skin...

Notes on Contributors

MARTIN ANDERSON spent many years living and teaching in the Far East before returning to his native England. His most recent collections are *Obsequy for Lost Things* and *Ice Stylus* (Shearsman Books, 2014 and 2017).

DARAGH BREEN's recent collection, *What the Wolf Heard*, was published by Shearsman Books in 2016. He lives in Cork, Ireland.

IAN BRINTON is the editor of three volumes of essays for Shearsman Books—two on J.H. Prynne and one on Peter Hughes—and is currently working on another Prynne volume. His translations of Yves Bonnefoy and Philippe Jaccottet have been widely published.

CARMEN BUGAN was born in 1970 in Romania and has since lived in the US, Ireland, England, and France. She is the author of three collections of poems, including *The House of Straw* and *Releasing the Porcelain Birds* from Shearsman Books, as well as the highly acclaimed memoir *Burying the Typewriter: Childhood Under the Eye of the Secret Police* (Picador), and a critical study entitled *Seamus Heaney and East European Poetry in Translation: Poetics of Exile* (MHRA/Legenda). Carmen teaches at the Gotham Writers Workshop in New York City and lives on Long Island, NY.

SUSIE CAMPBELL is the author of two chapbooks, *The Bitters* (Dancing Girl Press, 2014) and *The Frock Enquiry* (Annexe, 2015). Her work was included in the 2017 Museum of Futures' avant-garde visual poetry exhibition and she performed on behalf of Writers at Risk at the 2017 English PEN Modern Literature Festival.

CHLOE CARNEZI, born 1996, is a Greek undergraduate student of English at the University of Exeter. She is passionate about capturing contemporary Greek identity through poetry and prose. These are her first published poems.

RACHAEL CLYNE lives in Glastonbury. Her collection *Singing at the Bone Tree* is published by Indigo Dreams. Magazine appearances include: *Tears in the Fence*, *Prole*, *The Rialto*, *Under the Radar*, *The Interpreter's House*.

CATHY DREYER lives in Oxfordshire and is studying under Philip Gross for an M.Phil at the University of South Wales.

STEVE ELY is a poet from the West Riding of Yorkshire. His book of poems, *Oswald's Book of Hours*, is published by Smokestack and was nominated for the Forward Prize for Best First Collection in 2013 and the Ted Hughes Award for New Work in Poetry in 2014. *Englaland*, his second collection, was published by Smokestack in 2015. His novel, *Ratmen*, is published by

Blackheath Books. *Ted Hughes's South Yorkshire: Made in Mexborough*, a biographical work about Hughes's neglected Mexborough period, was published by Palgrave MacMillan in 2015.

Liam Ferney's most recent collection, *Content*, was shortlisted for the Queensland Poetry Prize. His previous collection, *Boom*, was shortlisted for the NSW Premier's and Queensland poetry prizes. His work has been widely published internationally and translated into Korean and Chinese. He lives in Brisbane.

Eiffel Gao is a Chinese poet currently doing a Creative Writing MA at Durham University. Her poems have appeared in *Transect Magazine*.

David Hadbawnik is a scholar of Medieval Literature who teaches at present in Kuwait. His translation of the *Aeneid,* Books I-VI, was published by Shearsman Books in 2015. We hope to publish the remaining six books in due course.

Lucy Hamilton co-edits *Long Poem Magazine* and works freelance for the Cambridge Rivers Project, King's College, Cambridge. Her collection *Stalker* (Shearsman 2012), was shortlisted for the Forward's Felix Dennis Prize for Best First Collection, and was chosen as a core set book on a new 'Creative Writing Life Writing' course at the University of Chester 2016/17. Her next collection, *Relatives and Other Explorers*, will be published by Shearsman Books in early 2018. Work-in-progress explores her extended family—history, geography, mythology—through photo-collages and the poems written about them afterwards. Recent poetry and artwork have appeared in *Artemis, Long Exposure, Ink, Sweat & Tears* and *The Wolf.*

Andrew Houwen is a translator of Dutch and Japanese poetry and is currently a JSPS post-doctoral fellow at Tokyo Woman's Christian University. Some of his translations from the Dutch poet Esther Jansma were read at the 2013 Reading Poetry Festival and subsequently published in *Modern Poetry in Translation* and *Shearsman*. His own poetry has appeared in the *Oxonian Review.*

Philippe Jaccottet (1925-) is one France's (and Switzerland's, for he was born in that country) finest living poets, and is only the fifteenth living author to be included in the prestigious Bibliothèque de la Pléiade. A number of his books have been translated into English, including *Seedtime* (trans. Lefevere & Hamburger, New Directions, New York), *Under Clouded Skies & Beauregard* (trans. Constantine & Treharne, Bloodaxe Books), *Selected Poems* (trans. Mahon, Penguin Books & Wake Forest University Press), *Second Seedtime* (trans. Lewis, University of Chicago Press) & *And, Nonetheless: Selected Prose and Poetry 1990-2009* (trans. Taylor, Chelsea Editions, New York).

HO CHEUNG LEE lives in Hong Kong, where he teaches and writes. He earned his Ed.D from the University of Hong Kong with a thesis on teaching reading. He is the founding editor of *BALLOONS Lit. Journal*. His poetry and short stories have appeared in *Eunoia Review, Poetry Quarterly, River Poet Journal, Sierra Nevada Review, The Chaffey Review, The Interpreter's House, The Oddville Press, The Writing Disorder*, and elsewhere. His poetry was shortlisted in Oxford Brookes University's International Poetry Competition (2016) and also for the erbacce-prize for poetry (2017). His photography and artwork have appeared in *Rattle* and *Typehouse Literary Magazine*, both as cover art, and also in **82 Review, Front Porch Review* and *The Adirondack Review*.

JOHN LEVY is a retired attorney and public defender living in Tucson, Arizona, and was a contributing editor to the very first series of this magazine in 1981-1982. His books include *Oblivion, Tyrants, Crumbs* (Tel-Let, 2003), *Scribble & Expanse* (Tel-Let, 1995), *We Don't Kill Snakes Where We Come From* (Querencia Press, 1994). A recent e-book, *In the Pit of the Empty*, is available on the Otata blog and includes one of the poems here: https://otatablog. files.wordpress.com/2016/12/levy-in-the-pit-of-the-empty2.pdf

OSIP MANDELSTAM (1891-1938), who fell afoul of Stalin in the 1930s and died in a transit camp on his way to imprisonment in the Gulag, was one of the greatest Russian poets of the 20th century. Initially associated with the Acmeists, he wrote the movement's manifesto. He published two collections during his own lifetime, as well as memoirs, essays and other prose, but the majority of his work was memorised by his widow, Nadezhda, and thus preserved, to be published only following the artistic thaw of the 1960s.

JULIE MACLEAN lives in Australia. Her latest publications include *Lips that Did* (Dancing Girl Press, 2017) and a collaboration with UK poet Terry Quinn, *To Have To Follow* (Indigo Dreams Publishing, 2016). Her work appears in *The Best Australian Poetry* (UQP) and *POETRY* (Chicago). She blogs at www.juliemacleanwriter.com

ALISTAIR NOON is a poet and translator living in Berlin. He has published a number of poetry chapbooks over the years including *Surveyors' Riddles* (Sidekick Books 2015), a collaboration with the poet Giles Goodland. He has also published two full-length collections with Nine Arches Press—*Earth Records* in 2012, which was shortlisted for the Michael Murphy Memorial Prize, and a follow-up, *The Kerosone Singing* in 2015.

NAKA TARŌ (1922-2014) was a post-war Japanese poet and winner of the Saisei Murō and Yomiuri poetry prizes. His poetry is characterised by its wordplay and its mixture of avant-garde techniques and allusions to Buddhism and classical Japanese literature. In addition to his poetry, he has written a Nō play, *Shikōtei* ('Shi Huangdi', 2003), and is also known for his critical work on Hagiwara Sakutarō.

NIHEI CHIKAKO has recently completed a doctoral thesis on the novels of Murakami Haruki at the University of Sydney. She is currently a lecturer at Yamaguchi University in Japan and is working on a publication concerning Murakami and literary translation.

Most recently JOHN PHILLIPS is the author of *Shape of Faith* from Shearsman Books. Previously he has published *Language Is* (Sardines Press), *What Shape Sound* (Skysill Press) and *Heretic* (Longhouse Publishers).

CLAIRE POTTER is an Australian poet living in London and currently working on her second manuscript (from which these poems printed here are taken). She has published two chapbooks and one full-length collection, *Swallow* (Five Islands Press, Melbourne). Most recently, she has had a poem and an essay published in *Poetry* (Chicago) as well as a poem in *Poetry Ireland Review* and *Best Australian Poems 2016*.

DAVID RUSHMER lives in Cambridge, UK. His works have appeared in *Angel Exhaust, Archive of the Now, Blaze VOX, Epizootics, E.ratio, Great Works, Molly Bloom, Oasis, OxMag, pen:umbra, Shearsman, Tremblestone* and *10th Muse*.

HELEN TOOKEY lives in Liverpool and teaches creative writing at Liverpool John Moores University. Her first full-length collection, *Missel-Child*, was published by Carcanet in 2014 and shortlisted for the Seamus Heaney prize (2015). Her pamphlet *In the Glasshouse* was published by HappenStance in 2016.

VIRGIL was the national poet of ancient Rome. *The Aeneid* was his magnum opus, left unfinished—but very nearly complete—when he died.